Victorian Village Life:
A Warwickshire Schoolmaster's Record

by Anne Langley
Stretton on Dunsmore, Warwickshire, England

Copyright 2004 © Stretton on Dunsmore History Society.
Published by Stretton Millennium History Group.
Scanning, page make-up and design by Warwick Dipple Design, Rugby.
Printed in England by Emmersons, Kenilworth.
Both cover pictures are reproduced from page 18 of *My Pretty Gift Book*, published by the
Religious Tract Society and given to my grandfather, Jack Lovatt, in 1879.

Copies of this book can be obtained from local outlets or ordered from
12 Squires Road, Stretton on Dunsmore, Rugby, CV23 9HF. Please enclose a cheque for £3.50
made out to Stretton History Society and an A5 stamped addressed envelope (postage 75g).
Details of other publications are on page 32.

ISBN 0-9537462-2-4

Victorian Village Life:
A Warwickshire Schoolmaster's Record

by Anne Langley
Stretton on Dunsmore, Warwickshire, England

This book is dedicated to the schoolmasters, Mr Leech, Mr Walker and Mr Hassall, who recorded a lively picture of village life in their school logbooks.

Contents

Stretton on Dunsmore

This booklet describes life in a Warwickshire village in the second half of the nineteenth century. It is based on contemporary records, especially the logbooks kept by the schoolmasters in Stretton on Dunsmore from 1862 onwards, and most quotations in the booklet are from this source. The village lies between Coventry and Rugby, near where the Fosse Way crosses the A45. In Victorian times it was a community of around 600 people with a green at the heart where the post office and main shops were situated. Rows of cottages radiated out from the centre, with a few larger buildings: the Manor House, the Vicarage and several farmhouses. There was an Anglican Church, a Primitive Methodist Chapel and a village school, two pubs near the centre (The Oak & Black Dog and The Shoulder of Mutton) with two more (The Dun Cow and The White Lion) on the London Road (now the A45) to cater for coaches and other traffic passing by. The moat shown on the map (now filled in) may have been a fishpond or a garden feature. There were various small quarries in or near the village for extracting gravel, clay, limestone and gypsum (used to make plaster), together with the related brickworks and lime kiln.

Figure 1 Map of Stretton on Dunsmore in the late nineteenth century

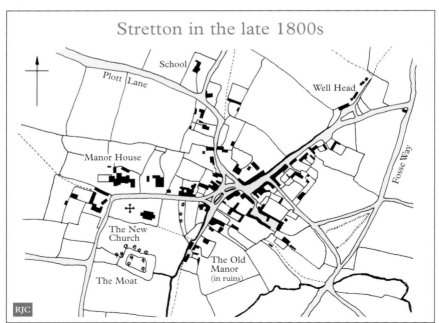

Living in a Victorian Village

Life in a Victorian village was very different from today with no electricity, gas or running water. Homes had no refrigerator, vacuum cleaner or washing machine (although early versions were invented towards the end of this period); and of course there were no televisions, computers or mobile phones. Cameras and bicycles were a rarity until the very end of the nineteenth century. With no cars, local transport relied almost entirely on the horse although there were trains. So what would it have been like to live then?

The agricultural labourer's wife

Imagine you're a woman living in Stretton a little over 150 years ago; it's 1851 and the enumerator has just filled in the census form because neither you nor your husband can read or write. You live in The Plott, a hamlet on the outskirts of the village, in a small thatched cottage lit by candles. The privy is a hut down the garden, shared with your neighbours. There's an open fire in the kitchen so you have to gather kindling regularly. You cook over this fire and get up early once a week to heat water in a copper for washing clothes. You fetch drinking water from a communal pump and collect rainwater in a butt for washing.

You've had nine children, five of whom have survived; thank goodness breast-feeding seems to stop new babies coming for a couple of years. The cottage needs cleaning every day, because the fire makes a

> 'St. Swithin's day, very hot and no rain... The school pumps & most of the pumps in the village dry' (July 1878).

lot of dust and your husband works on a farm and he and the children tramp mud into the house. He earns 10 shillings a week; you work part-time as a charwoman in order to earn a few more shillings a week. The village has a grocer, a butcher and a baker but storing food is a problem so you have to shop daily in warm weather.

There's a little school in the village but you can't see the point in sending the children because it's not compulsory, costs money and they'd need clean clothes and boots. So you send your children out to work as soon as you can. The boys start doing odd jobs for farmers when they're seven, and go to work as ploughboys full-time a few years later. The girls help with the baby and housework, and start winding silk to earn a few pennies as soon as they're old enough (first at home and then in the local silk mill). If your husband's ill and off work or dies there's no pension and no benefits, and of course you've got no savings. You'll be evicted from your cottage if you can't afford the rent (which is 1 shilling a week). You might take in a lodger or try to find another husband but that could be difficult because you look much older than your years. One or both of you will probably end up in the workhouse in Rugby; your husband in the men's side and you in the women's.

Figure 2 Stretton village centre in the 1900s: Mr. Borsley's grocery and Moor Farm

The skilled worker

Now suppose you're a carpenter living in a bigger house near the centre of the village. You inherited the house from your father and have turned an outbuilding into your workshop; you're very proud of your (foot-operated) lathe and tools. You turn your hand to various odd jobs around the village as well as 'proper' carpentry. You went to school for a few years and can read and write just enough to sort out the accounts. You've got one apprentice – a growing lad who eats you out of house and home. You walk everywhere, renting a cart when you need it to collect wood or deliver furniture. You enjoy a pint in a local pub where you meet the men you grew up with, and have a bit put by in the Friendly Society.

You won't hear of your wife going out to work because a woman's place is in the home – even when times are hard and you could use the money. And she's got a family of seven to care for. The children go to the village school and then at 12 years old the boys will be apprenticed to a trade and the girls go into service until they get married. Your wife may do a bit of dressmaking for friends as the children get older, and she has a bit more time, but you wouldn't dream of mentioning this on the census form you've just filled in. You have goods delivered from the local shops, and when you need something else your wife goes to Coventry with the carter on market day. You keep a pig in the back yard to help feed the family all winter and grow vegetables on an allotment, whilst your wife grows flowers such as tiger lilies and roses in the garden.

The People

Many individuals are mentioned in the logbooks over the years. The local gentry appear as benefactors, giving the children teas and other treats. In the 1890s Squire Rose supplied soup to the school twice a week during the winter months, Captain Lister-Kaye sent a quantity of periodicals down from the Manor House and the children had half-holidays so they could attend the marriage of his daughters, Miss Hermione and Miss Violet. The gentry had servants and a governess for the girls whilst the boys went away to boarding school. It was still a pretty feudal system, even in an 'open' village like Stretton that was not dependant on one large estate for its existence.

The local tradesmen also appear regularly, such as the grocer (Mr. Borsley) and the butcher (Mr. Wilcox); in February 1888 two of their children got married: 'Marriage of William Wilcox & Charlotte Borsley at half past one. School did not meet till after two o'clock... Semi-choral service'. Mr. Borsley is seen standing outside his shop on the village green in Figure 2. He became a trustee of the school and visited regularly to check the registers, distribute prizes, announce half-holidays and mark the new millennium in 1900.

The struggle to clothe a family

'Mrs. K. came about her boy being sent back [for clean clothes]. She declared that she could not get any clothes, & that if she filled the bellies of her children it is all that can be expected of her. I said I had given many clothes to the family, but I could not clothe all her children. Last week I gave the younger K.s an armful of clothing' (December 1889).

Many of the male villagers were agricultural labourers; in the early part of the Victorian period they would have protected their clothes by wearing a smock. Women wore pinafores, with a shawl in cold weather and a bonnet against the sun. Children wore boots; boys had caps with jackets and knee-length trousers and girls wore hats with pinafores over dresses; very young boys also wore a dress. In the logbooks we hear of children excused going to church because of torn clothes or old boots. Poor villagers wore second-hand clothes and didn't wash much. The schoolmaster complained about some of the children: 'The smell from their clothes is sometimes unbearable, and renders them unfit to sit with clean children. Now the cold weather has come, the stench from their clothes when sent to the fire to warm themselves fills the school, and it would be hard if they were never allowed to go to the fire'. We imagine a golden age when children respected their elders but it wasn't all like that: for instance Henry O. defied his father and often slept in barns at night. He played truant, was idle in his school work, and gave the Attendance Officer a great deal of trouble; the schoolmaster suggested he should be sent to a 'truant school'.

Work

The village contained several farms producing chiefly wheat, beans and turnips, and the majority of the men living locally worked on these farms. Others were craftsmen in such disappearing trades as blacksmith, cooper (barrel-maker), cordwainer (shoemaker), hurdle-maker, saddler and wheelwright. There were several shopkeepers and publicans, a few professionals – chiefly the vicar and the schoolteachers – and the gentry including the principal local landowners. The box below shows some of the occupations in Stretton in 1866. Little had changed in the work of this rural community for hundreds of years apart from the new job of postmistress. During the Victorian era, however, the industrial revolution finally arrived locally and some villagers started working on the railway or at the silk mill a few miles away in Brandon.

Extract from Morris's Warwickshire Trade Directory 1866
Stretton on Dunsmore: Trades and Professions

Adkins Thomas, wheelwright	Cleaver Richard, beer retailer
Allistone Richard, "Shoulder of Mutton"	Elkington James, farmer
Amos Charles, saddler	Falkner Joseph, carrier
Barnett William, tailor	Goddard Thomas, baker
Blundell Mrs Mary, blacksmith	Hobday James, shoemaker
Borsley David, grocer	Hobday Mrs. Mary, drill maker
Claridge Edward, cooper	Quiney Miss Esther, farmer
Claridge Thomas, hurdle maker	Taylor Mrs Maria, Post Office
Clark Robert, bricklayer	Wilcox Thomas, butcher

Victorian farming was badly affected by free trade and competition from cheap foreign imports, particularly corn. The consequent agricultural depression started around 1870 and lasted well into the twentieth century. Mechanization added to the woes of the worker, as machines replaced men. The school logbooks reflect these problems, with families struggling to pay their school fees and very young children being sent out to work. The decline of the silk-ribbon industry in nearby Coventry exacerbated the situation after 1860; many weavers were forced to starve or emigrate and so there were few opportunities locally for unemployed agricultural labourers. The Tolpuddle martyrs had been transported in 1834 for forming an Agricultural Union, which put paid to activity for nearly 40 years until Joseph Arch founded the National Agricultural Labourers' Union in 1872. There were signs of early trade union activity in Stretton: 'Many absent for two or three days on account of the Labourers Union tea meeting' (June 1872). Itinerant labour helped with the main corn harvest: the schoolboys were reproved for insulting Irish reapers one August. The workers in the picture opposite were laying drainage pipes on the Duke of Buccleuch's estate in Dunchurch (he owned land in Stretton too).

Figure 3 Farm workers in Dunchurch in the 1890s

Most women in Victorian Stretton worked in a limited range of 'female' occupations: servant, charwoman, washerwoman, dressmaker, nurse or teacher. Others worked on the land or in the local silk industry. There were several women farmers, a postmistress and a female blacksmith, most of whom had inherited the business from a male relative. Women working affected the children: 'Elder children are being kept at home to take care of babies while the mothers go out to gather the peas' (July 1890).

Child labour
Children went out to work very young. The youngest child mentioned in the Stretton school logbooks was a six-year-old sent to work, and the 1851 census records a seven-year-old chimney sweep in nearby Wolston, but it is likely that even younger children were working in the first half of the nineteenth century. The importance of child labour was demonstrated by the month's closure of the school for 'Harvest holyday'; the timing depended on the ripening corn and in one very wet year the start was delayed until September 11th. The commonest work for boys was in agriculture, sowing and harvesting crops, with a seasonal pattern that affected attendance at school as shown in the chart below; the most frequently mentioned occupations being underlined. On one occasion a boy took a pig to be 'hogged' (castrated). Long-term absentees only attended school in winter when there was less work available.

Month	Work causing absence from school
January	Crow scaring.
February	Planting crops: <u>setting wheat & beans</u>, pea dropping, crow scaring, tending sheep.
March	Setting wheat, beans & potatoes, dropping peas, plough driving.
April	<u>Setting potatoes</u>, oats & barley, stone picking, weeding, tending sheep, plough driving.
May	Potato setting.
June	<u>Pea gathering</u>, hay making.
July	Hay making, harvesting corn, gleaning, crow scaring.
August	<u>Harvesting corn</u>, gleaning.
September	<u>Gleaning</u>, tending pigs, gathering potatoes, apples & blackberries.
October	<u>Gathering acorns</u> & potatoes, setting wheat, tending pigs.
November	<u>Setting wheat</u>, gathering sticks.
December	Pig killing, crow scaring, beating for hunters.

Girls were mentioned less frequently in the logbooks, but some were absent gimping* (winding silk[1]), bead-threading*, working at home, at the silk mill or as servants with a local family. They occasionally worked on farms: Edward and Esther Boneham were both planting wheat on Church Farm one year. Political correctness had not yet been invented. Some words and attitudes would be unacceptable today: 'Mrs. Robbins wishes her daughter to sew every afternoon as she is a cripple & will in all probability have to get her living by sewing. Under the circumstances I have no objection if the Trustees will allow it' (June 1871). Paper girls and boys were employed: 'Two of Parrott's children are required to leave at 3.30 to meet a train for newspapers which they sell every evening' (June 1892). Children, particularly girls, were also kept away by their parents: running errands, helping round the house or minding the baby whilst their mother did the washing. The school also took very young children (from the age of three) whilst the mother worked.

The schoolmaster often complained of boys who were regularly absent, some for long periods. 'J. Washbrooke & E. Robbins reappeared after more than a year's absence. This owing to the policeman serving warning upon the farmers' (February 1876). The master had to fill out a 'Factory book' to record the children working in Brandon silk mill, which caused problems over a 30-year period. There was regular contact with the local Attendance Officer Mr. Root (who was also Relieving Officer for the Poor Law Authorities). Once the schoolmaster received an anonymous letter stating that Herbert Burbery was often employed illegally at the Vicarage!

[1] *Words marked * are explained in the Glossary at the end of this booklet.*

We can sympathise with parents sending children out to work when the father was earning as little as ten shillings a week. The situation for those out of work, or working part-time, was even worse, and many of the school-age children who worked in Stretton came from single-parent families. The schoolmasters were sympathetic to the plight of some families: 'Rosa O. (11) is required at home to nurse the baby now that its mother is dead' (July 1883).[2] 'Allowed William Smith to go to work for a time on account of the destitute state of the family – seven children, not one at work & father often out of work' (October 1885). 'George K... shews signs of starvation. His brain is very feeble, his face very pale, & father out of work. They have been gathering mushrooms & selling them. There is a large family with only two boys out at work' (October 1887). The schoolmaster shrewdly analysed the problem: 'Men out of work go acorning and take their children with them. Why are they out of work? Because the farmers find that boys at 12 years of age can do a man's work. How so? Because he has been apprenticed to agricultural work since he was about 8 years old & is now doing a man's work for a boy's money' (October 1870).

Some of the legislation affecting child labour	
1788	Chimney Sweepers Act (others Acts followed in 1834 & 1840).
1819	Cotton Mills Act (and another Act in 1825).
1833	A Factory Act stopped children up to age 8 working in textile factories and limited 9- to 13-year-olds to working 8 hours a day.
1842	A Mines Act prevented boys under 10 from working underground.
1844	Children working in textile factories had to spend 3 days a week, or 6 half days, in school (later this was extended to other factories).
1847	The Ten Hours Act stopped women and children working longer hours.
1867	The Agricultural Gangs Act prohibited children under the age of 8 working in Agriculture (this was raised to the age of 10 in 1873).
1904	Half-time schooling was abolished by Warwickshire County Council.

Legislation was gradually enacted to prevent the appalling exploitation of young children in mines, factories and elsewhere. Child labour in nineteenth-century Stretton was chiefly the result of poverty caused by low adult wages, irregular work, unemployment or the loss of a parent. The 1881 census recorded a substantial reduction in child labour in Stretton, suggesting that the nineteenth-century Factory and Education legislation had been effective. However, the census figures represent only the tip of the iceberg of child labour described in the school logbooks. There were attendance problems even after schooling became compulsory in 1880, though the situation improved somewhat once it became free in 1891. Even so attendance problems persisted into the twentieth century when demand for boys' labour was so high that 'Farmers are employing two half-timers alternately' (September 1901).

[2] *Rosa. Henry's sister, was the neice of the unfortunate Mrs O. mentioned on page 28.*

The Village School

The first school in Stretton was founded in 1789 using money from public subscriptions and the charitable bequest of William Herbert (see Figure 10, page 25). This school provided free education for poor children; the first teacher, Miss Mary Mason, was paid 10 guineas* a year. The original curriculum was very practical – children being taught to read, sew, knit and spin – though by 1850 they were also taught writing and arithmetic. In 1862 an Inspector described the old schoolrooms as 'low, ill-ventilated and inconveniently arranged'. Later that year a new Victorian Gothic school was opened (see picture below). This building cost £1,145 to build and was used for over a hundred years; you can see the schoolmaster's house on the left.

Figure 4 Stretton school, teachers and children around 1900

In this new National School boys and girls were taught separately at first: one boy was lectured for sending a note to a girl through the folding-doors. After a few years Her Majesty's Inspector recommended that they be taught together because the girls were falling behind in arithmetic. Miss Johnson, very experienced but uncertificated, clearly resented being relegated to teaching the infants and needlework, and fought a rearguard action to try to delay or sabotage the eventual integration. The schoolmaster found the girls 'very dull' when he took them over in 1870, and it was a few years before they caught up with the boys. The school had up to 147 children, over half of them in the Infant School, and most left as soon as they legally could.

School dinners were not provided: children went home in the long lunch break or brought food to eat outside in summer and inside in winter. Soup was introduced twice a week during very cold weather in 1886 and cost 1d a time. 'They bring basins and spoons and eat it in the desks' (January 1888). Some children cheekily treated it like a soup kitchen: 'Some who are not present at school on the day, yet come for the soup' (February 1891).

Fees were charged at the National School: in January 1865 it cost 1½ pence per week, with an additional charge for copybooks for writing. Some parents tried barter: 'Two boys, C. Howkins & Thos. Howkins, sent home for their School Fees. They brought Peach instead of 1½ each' (April 1867). The schoolmaster resorted to cash incentives for a while, paying a penny to children who attended regularly, and prizes for attendance and good work were given out annually from 1877 onwards. Families who sent a child to school were caught in a double bind: they lost the child's earnings and also had to pay school fees. One master summarised the problem: 'The poorer classes will not deny themselves for the sake of the education of their children. Nor can they be reasonably expected to do so when 10 shillings per week is all they obtain for their labour' (October 1870). Schooling did not become free until 1891.

Some of the legislation affecting Victorian schools	
1870	Forster's Education Act paved the way for national elementary schooling; details were left to local bye-laws.
1876	'Leaving' or 'Labour certificates' were introduced for children who had reached a certain age, or attended regularly, and achieved a set standard.
1880	An Education Act made schooling from the ages of 5-10 compulsory; children under the age of 13 could leave with a certificate.
1891	Elementary Schooling was provided free.
1893	The leaving age went up to 11 (and to 12 in 1899).

The Teachers

Mr. Leech started teaching at Stretton in 1861; he was clearly a kind young man, who agonised over his work and struggled to persuade the boys to turn up, to learn the 3 Rs and to behave in a civilized manner. For this he earned £60 a year, plus a few extras and a house that went with the job. Mr. Walker took over in 1867 and he in turn was succeeded by Mr. Hassall who taught at Stretton for over 30 years (from 1872-1906). The schoolmaster had an uneasy relationship with parents. His was a strange role, not quite fully professional, but definitely a cut above the trading classes and artisans. He was both the master and the servant of the people in the village; he was a respected person but also at the beck and call of the Vicar and his family. He issued the vouchers for charity club handouts but also had to persuade parents to produce their children on time, clean and properly dressed with their school fees.

The master regularly visited homes to encourage attendance at school, particularly when an inspection was due. Later on he reported parents to the Attendance Officer if children were persistently absent. For instance, Emma and George K. did not come to the Examination: 'The first had no books, the second was naked in the coal-hole and refused to come out & put on his clothes' (February 1886). Parents were sometimes rude and uncooperative; one mother came into the playground, slapped a girl in the face and hit her with a pail. Very occasionally appreciation was recorded: 'Wet day...Master dried clothes. Mother gratified "Mr. Leech has children of his own"...Boy's Mother at School expressed satisfaction at Son's and grandson's progress' (October and November 1865).

Mr Leech requested a pupil-teacher in March 1865 but this was refused and a monitor appointed instead: monitors were trusted senior pupils who were responsible to the schoolmaster and paid £2 a year. They had little or no training but performed a useful role helping the master to teach up to 80 children in one room; by 1873 there were six monitors. There are occasional comments on their teaching: 'The monitor Thompson commended for good teaching' (October 1869). They were expected to set a good example: 'Boy deposed from monitorship for disobedience to Widowed Mother' (June 1866). They sometimes got up to mischief: '4 boys and Monitor punished for putting Spiders into Ale barrels in lobby' (September 1866); presumably the ale was for the master and not the boys. A bright child could move into the profession of teaching by becoming a monitor and then a pupil-teacher: 'J. Borsley [a monitor] to go as pupil teacher in Rugby' (July 1875). Pupil-teachers had to be 13 years old and were instructed by the master; they earned between £10 and £20 a year and after four or five years could take an entrance examination for teacher training college. Mr. Hassall's own children, mainly girls, provided a seemingly inexhaustible supply of monitors who progressed to pupil teacher, assistant teacher (paid £35 a year), college and then teacher in local schools.

Emily Boneham was christened Mary Emily in Stretton in March 1861. Sadly her mother died when she was only four and she was sent to school; later her father remarried. She was clearly a girl of spirit: in July 1870 she was 'reproved for inattention & lying. I sent her back to correct a sum, she sat idle for 10 minutes & then brought it up saying she could find no mistake. I had watched her & knew therefore that she was simply idle'. In January the following year Emily 'refused to come into the Boys' School at her father's bidding. I compelled her to come in (or as an alternative to leave the Girls' School)'. She reached Standard VI and became a monitor in December 1872. The next month: 'Sent E. Boneham, Monitor to her place in her class & would not allow her to teach this week for putting ink on the children's faces'. Emily left school at the age of 15 and became a domestic servant; she married Edmund Hopcraft, a railway clerk in Rugby, and they had three children.

The curriculum in 1862 included reading, writing, arithmetic, scripture, history and geography, with sewing for the girls. A harmonium was purchased for £10 to assist with music lessons; drill and exercises are mentioned occasionally. 'Object lessons' were introduced in the 1870s to show children pictures of unfamiliar things such as rice, a crocodile and a whale. Mr. Hassall introduced Latin and French with an 'Advanced Class' for a few years, but this fell victim to the demands of the rigid national curriculum and 'payment by results': the government grant was based on attendance figures and the children's achievements against set standards in given subjects. In 1891 a grant was offered for Technical Education; the Master was keen but the Trustees 'decided to have nothing to do with it' (February 1891). Later in the year, however: 'Boys who have left school are to be taught Carpentry & Drawing.' Teaching was very rigid, with rows of desks, lots of repetition and copying, and little opportunity for self-expression. Slates were used for much of the work and reluctantly consigned to history in 1905.

Figure 5 A typical village classroom at Hartshill in the early twentieth century.

Night school classes were held three evenings a week during the winter months (from October until March). Attendance fluctuated considerably, but was usually around a dozen, all boys; very occasionally adults joined them. The master was paid extra for teaching the night school, which occupied a couple of hours, starting at 7.15 p.m. It disappeared when education became compulsory. There was also a Sunday school in the village attended by about 50 children. In the first half of the nineteenth century more children were educated in Sunday Schools than National Schools, because the former were free, and children could still earn money during the week; the education offered was however very limited, with a strong focus on scripture.

The Children

Children started at five years old in the infants' school and there were very few over ten in the 1860s. They regularly arrived dirty: 'Sent home 2 boys for clean pinafores... Boy, again sent home to wash and comb, came back very tidy – clean smock' (October 1862). The logbook also records absence because of clothes needing to be washed or repaired, or torn through bird-nesting. 'Weather very sharp, with snow. Two or three of the children are really not sufficiently clad to come through it' (December 1892). We get an insight into the way they normally talked from an entry in the logbook about ungrammatical phrases: 'I ain't got none' and 'Are I to shew them?'

Their behaviour left much to be desired: 'Two boys punished for drawing horses, ferrets, dogs etc. on desk... Boy punished for bad language. Ditto using Lane instead of Urinal' (March and October 1865). Boys were also punished for: stealing, falsehood, blasphemy, playing or irreverence at prayers, singing an obscene song, imitating the master, meddling with provision bags in the lobby, not hastening home in the rain, fighting, striking a lady with a stick or throwing a stone at a man on horseback. Punishments included lecturing, boxing ears, slapping the face, using a cane on the hand, shoulder or back (and fingers and head by mistake). Serious punishments had to be recorded, initially in the logbook, and later in a punishment book. Girls got up to mischief and were caned as well as boys.

> **Matthew Wing** was born in Kersley and admitted to school at the age of seven; in July he was 'eating unripe plums – sent word to Mother'. In January 1867 he 'found 6d lost the day before' and in October: 'M. Wing returns from pig tending'. In April 1868: 'Mat Wing goes to work. Must call on parent.' The call was clearly successful as he was back in school for the examinations in May, aged 11, when he obtained 65% and passed Standard II in Reading, Writing and Arithmetic. That is the last we hear of Matthew in the logbooks but census records show him as a 12-year old ploughboy living with his parents and four siblings in Clay Pit Cottage; as an agricultural labourer married to Rebekah living in a cottage in Princethorpe, and by 1901 as a general labourer living in Coventry with his wife, her mother and their six children.

Mr. Leech tried hard to teach the children kindness to animals. He rebuked the boys for killing butterflies and 'a little boy killing a toad with a stick' (May 1866). The year before an injured bird was brought to him in May, a bird sold to him in June and he forbade the bringing of nestlings to school in a box in July. He objected to robbing birds' nests but had an uphill struggle, with little support for his ideas: 'Father of boy called on me about Son [reported to the Vicar for meddling with a sparrow's nest in the School-eaves] had no strong objection to bird-nesting' (June 1866). Some creatures were less welcome: 'The work of this day much interfered with by wasps constantly

entering the room through the open windows' (August 1890). Mr. Hassall gave a
practical demonstration of leaf structure: 'The ribs and veins I illustrated by means of a
Rhubarb leaf out of the garden, holding it up to the light between the window & the
children, which showed the network of veins admirably' (June 1900).

It was not all hard work at school, the children sometimes had treats. Mr. Leech
brought in cake for the boys on his son's birthday in May 1863, and the following year
they were given currants in July, whilst in October the Vicar's daughter distributed
sweets and cakes and 'Apples given away for chair-fetching for service in School-room',
the church being shut for renovation.

Figure 6 Stretton children and teachers around 1900: Mr. Hassall on the right

Attendance was a perpetual 'struggle between Custom and Authority': 'Great
discouragement from the indifference of parents in sending their children to school,
e.g. gathering acorns, fetching pair of boots' (October 1862). The lack of schooling
showed up in literacy rates: 26% of Warwickshire bridegrooms and 36% of brides were
illiterate in 1860. Children worked illegally, full or part-time, because families were
hard up and employers wanted cheap labour. Many parents did not understand the
value of education so they sent school-age children out to work or kept them at home
to mind the baby. The School Attendance Officer chased up parents, who were
sometimes summoned and fined (usually 2s 6d) but this did not seem to deter them.
Things slowly improved after 1880 once education became compulsory.

Leisure

The chief leisure activity for many men in the village was drinking and socialising in one of the public houses that provided a meeting place for singing, games of skittles and dominoes, and self-help groups such as friendly societies. Cricket was mentioned occasionally (for example 'Cricket in Smith's field' July 1864). There were reports of a 'Penny reading'* at Wolston in October 1865, and in 1900 a 'Reading Room' was set up in a vacant house in the village. Seasonal events are shown in the box below. It should be mentioned that not everything occurred annually throughout the logbook period (1862-1906) so the average year was not quite as eventful as the list suggests.

Month	Leisure activities
January	Hunts
February	Valentine's Day, Shrove Tuesday pancakes, hunts
March	Hunts
April	All Fools Day, Rugby Races, Easter holiday
May	May Day, Whitsun, Coventry Fair & Lady Godiva* procession
June	Royal Agricultural Show, Band of Hope* fete
July	Dunchurch Wake, Eathorpe Flower Show & Wake*
August	Wolston, Brandon and Bourton Flower Shows, Wolston Wake, Allotment Rent Day, Potato Supper, Primrose League Fete,* Harvest holiday
September	Wolston Statutes,* Leamington Agricultural Show
October	Stretton Statutes, Michaelmas, Mop fairs*
November	Guy Fawkes Day, Wroth Silver* ceremony, hunts
December	Shoots, hunts, Christmas holiday

In January hunts met at pubs in local villages and children played truant to observe the spectacle; meets took place from November through to April, when farmers were less busy. On Shrove Tuesday in February: 'The pancakes at home kept many away. Half holiday in the afternoon according to custom' (1891). There is one mention of the post being very late on Valentine's Day and in 1890: 'every child present received either a book or a card kindly sent by the proprietors of Holloway's Pills & Ointment, & which was worth having'.

In March or April, Easter gave the children a short break but there is little reference in the logbooks to activities associated with Easter apart from: 'A concert... in which the girls of the 1st class acted "Wanted a servant", and some of the Infants "Grandpa" [an action song]' (1893). On April 1st Rugby Races were held; All Fools Day is mentioned but there is no reference to pranks associated with it. The boys did sometimes 'bar out' Mr. Leech by barricading the door, but this was usually on the last day of term.

Figure 7 Stretton May Day celebrations in 1905

The May Day celebrations to welcome spring were the highlight of that month. In the photo the school teacher, Mr. Hassall, can be seen with a hat and a white beard standing amongst the children. On the last day of April 1873 the children were 'out gathering flowers for tomorrow'. In 1893 they 'went all together with maypoles & collected over £3 which provided for them a tea, and 3d for each child'. The tea consisted of bread and butter, cake and an orange. In 1899: 'the teachers accompanied them in procession round the village singing May songs. Every child had a maypole, & Mrs. Wedge provided tea for them in the barn near her residence & after tea games'. The May Queen was elected by the children's votes for the first time in 1902; girls paraded the village with Maypoles and boys played football in the Hillies*. Mayday celebrations are widespread, ancient and possibly derived from pre-Christian fertility rites. Children still dance round a maypole in May and at the village fete in June.

The school closed for a week at Whitsun when Stretton Wake* was celebrated by a school tea party. The Coventry fair with the Lady Godiva* procession was held in various months (nowadays in June). For the school outing in June 1893: 'The Girls will take a journey to Meriden to-morrow. They will... be provided with tea etc. there. They pay 1/- each for the vehicles.' The Royal Agricultural Show was held at Warwick in June, another event that survives, now being held at Stoneleigh Abbey in early July.

In July the Band of Hope* Temperance fete was held at Leamington Hastings. In mid July there were Wakes* and flower shows. National bank holidays were introduced in 1871, and villagers started taking day trips during the late Victorian era, but most could not afford to go away on a week's holiday. There is one report in the logbooks of a family trip to the seaside, presumably by train: 'The stay at Scarborough of Beatrice & Maud Alcock has been cut short. They have returned to school this morning' (July 1895). In local villages on special occasions there were organised games for adults such as a tug of war, high jump, hurdle race, steeplechase, obstacle race, sack race, or climbing a greasy pole to obtain a leg of mutton.

In early August there was no school on the Allotment Rent Day and a half holiday for the Potato Supper. By 1869, the latter had been succeeded by the Allotment Supper held in September (forerunner of the modern Harvest Supper). During August there were more Wakes* and flower shows, Wolston Oddfellows walk,* and the Primrose League Fete*. One year a merry-go-round distracted the children. Mr. Hassall remarked rather sourly: 'I shall be glad when the "round of pleasures" is done' (August 1892).

In September there was the Leamington Agricultural Show and Wolston Statutes* at the end of the month. Stretton Statutes fair was held in mid October, around the time of 'Old Michaelmas' day and included a sheep roast. Along with Mothering Sunday, it was one of the few holidays for those in service: 'Old Michaelmas week, when boys & girls come home from service' (October 1894). This was also the time of the annual 'mop' fairs in Coventry and other places. Traditionally servants were hired by the year, and would stand at the fair with a symbol of their trade (e.g. a mop for domestic servants) waiting to be selected. Local Mop fairs still survive today in Warwick and Stratford on Avon. In September 1905 the Church Choir went on an outing to London, presumably by train.

In November the main event as far as the children were concerned was the bonfire on Guy Fawkes' Day, which brought a half holiday up until 1890: 'Boys gathering sticks &c. today' (1868). On November 11th: 'St. Martin's Day when "Wroth Silver"* is paid at Knightlow Hill before sunrise'; this 800-year old tradition still survives today. In the winter months there were shoots with a dozen boys 'beating' for the hunters. The children had a week or two for the Christmas holiday. There is surprisingly little mention of particular activities in relation to Christmas and no Nativity play, though they did sing carols. Once the Vicar requested the services of the Assistant Mistress to help decorate the Church and another year there is mention of decorating a tree in the Schoolroom after Christmas on January 15th. On January 1st one year there was a very small attendance in the afternoon because of 'Mrs Fuller's Xmas Tree and party'. The Christmas tree was a Victorian innovation, brought over from Germany by the royal family and gradually taken up in Britain.

Children's Games

Playground games

The teacher Mr. Hassall 'Taught the children the game of "Birds in a cage"..."Cats and Mice"..."Links in the Chain"...Set the girls off in the game of "Links in a Chain". They seem to have no heart to start a game themselves but stand around shivering' (October 1873).

Some of the less formal games the children played were also recorded in the school logbooks. The boys were playing pitch & toss (a gambling game) for buttons regularly in 1875. Some games were seasonal: in mid-April the top-spinning season succeeded to marbles (1866). Other activities depended on the weather: 'snowballing persons in Lane forbidden' (March 1866). Playing with a top or tip-cat* got the boys into trouble when it led to broken windows in the school. 'Florence Mawby going to a thin part of the play-ground fence to look at a passing musician fell through into the lane & injured her arm' (August 1892) and Louisa Ward sprained her ankle jumping over the brook. Organised games were held on occasions such as cricket on May Day 1900 and a football match against Bourton boys in November 1905.

Figure 8

Children playing leap-frog in Compton Wynyates village in the 1900s

Local and National Events

Village life was enlivened by a wide range of local events. There were sales at farms, inns or on the premises concerned, for example at the Brick Kiln in November 1864. Sporting events were held such as cricket matches. There was an Exhibition of Wild Beasts one year; elephants caused a stir in the village when they marched by on the London Road (now the A45) and the master noted the visit of Barnum & Bailey's Circus to Rugby and Coventry. News of important events in the locality was sometimes recorded: 'Warwick Castle burnt last Sunday – 1st in Advent' (December 1871).

Entertainments were held in the school because there was no village hall at that time, for example a musical entertainment or marionettes. As technology progressed there was 'a panorama or magic lantern show' (March 1893). Sometimes the individual entrepreneurs were named: Mr. Lawrence, Mr. Melon or Mr. Booth. The Bubbenhall Christie Minstrels sang (with blackened faces no doubt). Interesting people came to the village: 'a freed slave from the Southern States of America' gave an entertainment in November 1889 and the schoolmaster took the opportunity to explain about the American Civil War. A rather intriguing 'Galvanic lecture' was given in March 1865; this would have been a demonstration of electricity that was said to have healing powers. The master disapproved when: 'a conjurer from Leamington performed after school when above 100 children were present at 1d each'. A jumble sale was held in October 1897; two years later a choir concert and treat was held in April, a Sunday School tea party given by Mrs Lister-Kaye (of the Manor House) in July and a social evening in aid of the burial ground fund in November.

'The school used as a Polling Station for the first time in a General Election' (on a Thursday in July 1895). The vote had been given to most male householders by the Reform Bills of 1867 and 1884, but tenants were disenfranchised until 1918, and women until 1928. The Prince of Wales, the future Edward VII, visited Coventry in November 1874 and some children played truant to go and see the decorations in the city. Passers by would have been of more interest before the days of television: 'So many children had gone with their mothers to see some soldiers & cannon pass along the London Road, that I allowed the rest to go & see the sight' (July 1890).

The Temperance movement was strong in the area: during 1865 a Teetotal meeting was held at Wolston in March followed by a festival in June, tea-drinking in July and an 'Exhibition of Views' at Stretton Temperance Hall in November. The Temperance movement had strong links with Nonconformism; it aimed to recruit children to the Band of Hope* in order to prevent them drinking as adults. Local Band of Hope events recorded in the 1890s included dances, fetes, a festival and an annual outing to Stoneleigh Park in August.

National events had an impact too. Royal occasions were dutifully celebrated such as the wedding of the Royal Prince in March 1863 when the future King Edward VII married Princess Alexandra of Denmark. 'General holiday & public rejoicing on the occasion of the marriage of His Royal Highness Prince George with Princess May', the future King George V and Queen Mary (July 1893). Queen Victoria's Golden Jubilee was celebrated in 1887 with feasting, sports, fireworks and bonfires. For the Diamond Jubilee there was more 'Rejoicing' and a lime tree was planted on the green that still stands today.

Queen Victoria's Diamond Jubilee

The village was decorated with flags, festoons of evergreens and, near the dinner tent, the banner of the defunct Old Friendly Society, reminding many of happy gatherings in bygone days. Proceedings began with a hot dinner of roast and boiled beef and mutton, vegetables, and plum pudding [in June!] with unlimited supplies of ale and mineral waters. Long tables were laid under an awning of rick sheets, lent by the farmers and others, erected in the street, alongside the brook. The meat was cooked by Mr. W. Wilcox [the butcher] and the villagers boiled the vegetables, puddings &c. About 330 sat down to dinner at two o'clock; there were speeches and they sang the Old Hundredth and 'God Save the Queen', accompanied by the Marton Brass Band. A tea was given to 200 children and then they adjourned to a paddock where swings, roundabouts &c were erected. Sports included a sack race, a 3-legged race and 1/4 mile race for married men over 40; prizes ranged from 5s down to 6d. Parishioners then danced till ten o'clock. (From the *Rugby Advertiser*, July 3rd 1897)

For the coronation of Edward VII in 1902 the children had to practise singing God Save the King after over 50 years of God Save the Queen. 'Broke up for the Coronation Week. The King is to be crowned on Thursday next the 26th inst, but the Stretton festivities to be on Friday.' Then on June 30th: 'The King was not crowned on Thurs last as he was ill having gone under an operation for appendicitis, & his life in danger. The rejoicings at Stretton were postponed, & a Church Service held on Thursday to pray for his recovery.' On July 3rd, as the king was recovering, the Coronation festivities were held 'commencing at 4 o'clock with a tea for the children'. The coronation followed on August 9th.

During the Boer War, news of the relief of Ladysmith reached the village on March 1st 1900, the children were given a half-holiday and the church bells were rung. On May 17th news of the relief of Mafeking arrived and celebrations were held four days later: 'Holiday today, tea-drinking for the children of Stretton & Princethorpe, brass band & dancing in the evening in a field by the brookside lent by Mr. Coles.' Ten days later Mr. Borsley, now a school Trustee, informed the children that the British had entered Pretoria, President Kruger had fled and he gave them a half-holiday.

Illness

Infectious diseases spread rapidly around the village in Victorian times, because hygiene was lacking, food or water often contaminated and poor villagers could not afford treatment. The first Board of Health in the country was set up in Rugby in 1849, but it appears to have had little effect in the surrounding villages. There was no local surgery during the nineteenth century so villagers consulted the doctor in Marton: 'William Moss is kept at home, as he frequently is to go to the doctor's for Amelia's medicine' (August 1891). Sadly nine-year old Amelia died of consumption (tuberculosis) in November.

Dr. Wilson of Leamington, Medical Officer for the Rural Sanitary District, ordered the closure of the village school during epidemics: such as mumps (2 weeks during 1890), measles (2¹/₂ weeks in 1898) and scarlet fever (7 weeks in 1892). Scarlet fever was a killer then, and 21 children were kept

Figure 9 A cast-iron water pump still stands at The Plott in Stretton

away for ten days after the homes had been disinfected. Other diseases common amongst the children were chicken pox, and 'hooping' cough: 'some go red in the face with violent coughing at times'. Another interesting spelling is 'jaunders' for jaundice. Diphtheria and consumption were still a scourge; there were regular epidemics of typhoid fever and typhus, and an outbreak of small pox in 1871-2.

The master had a water pump installed in his scullery in 1865 but sanitation in the school was primitive: 'coal hovels' were installed in 1865 and dry earth closets in 1877. In 1883 a towel, bucket and soap were sent up from the grocery for the girls to wash their hands before needlework but the master feared it would encourage them to come to school with dirty hands. Running water was not installed until 1904 but Stretton was lucky: in 1957 there were still 44 Warwickshire schools without a water supply and/or drainage!

There are descriptions of what sounds like epilepsy: 'Herbert Ward had another fit. He is subject to them at times, & this makes him irritable & unable to attend to his work' (December 1893). There was one mention of St Vitus's Dance, writhing caused by a disorder of the brain. Children were described by the master as suffering from deranged bowels, vomiting or breaking out in the face. They were sent home when they came with lice, ringworm or bad sores on their faces or hands. Some of the illness was self-inflicted: one boy got 'sick through wine' and unripe crab apples were suspected as the source of stomach aches.

Accidents happened: a man cut his hand felling wood; a boy was shot in the leg – probably beating for a shoot as it was a Saturday. William Whitehead died after a bad fall from a swing; Mr. Hobday fell from a cart and broke his leg and 12-year old William Oakley was killed in the lane by a haywaggon. William Atkins' hand was smashed in a machine – probably for harvesting; 'Many cases of cut fingers, or gathered [infected] fingers... forbade attending till they can take a proper part' (October 1892). 'Willie Clark who was badly burnt last week in making a fire for his mother, died on Sunday from his injuries. This is the 3rd death of scholars this year' (November 1891). Mortality rates in Britain in the second half of the nineteenth century were high, and average life expectancy low, but this included a lot of infant deaths: a child who survived the first few years of life had a reasonable chance of living to old age. Even so the logbooks record a sad number of child deaths and details of unfortunate families: 'William K. [brother of Walter & George] has cut his hand; his mother is ill, & his brother wasting away of consumption' (May 1895).

There is the occasional report of an operation 'Edward Quartermain [a star pupil] is going to a hospital in Birmingham to have the guides of his eyes cut, so he will be absent several weeks' (November 1898); this sounds like an operation to correct a bad squint. Anaesthetics were introduced in the mid-nineteenth century and popularised by Queen Victoria who used chloroform in childbirth; but even so operations were frightening and dangerous events. It wasn't only people who fell ill: there was a service on account of cattle plague in March 1866. This disease (called rinderpest) was highly contagious and often fatal; bad outbreaks occurred throughout Britain during 1865-6.

Disease control in the nineteenth century

Water quality and sanitation gradually improved during this period, and though they still left much to be desired, the last major outbreak of cholera in Britain occurred in 1866. Public Health Acts intended to help control infectious diseases were introduced from 1848 onwards and compulsory vaccination (against smallpox) in 1853. Pasteur discovered that 'infective germs' caused disease around 1856 and disinfection was achieved by high heat or the use of antiseptics such as carbolic acid, developed by Lister in 1867.

Support for the Poor

Agricultural wages were always low and this period included the years of the 'Great Depression' of the 1870s with further distress in farming towards the end of the nineteenth century. At that period those who fell on hard times faced starvation, eviction and the humiliation of relying on charity or Poor Law relief. The new Poor Law, introduced in 1834, in theory abolished 'outdoor relief'* in favour of sending people to the workhouse (the Rugby Union Workhouse for Stretton). However there is evidence in the school logbooks that the local Poor Law Guardians supported people in the community throughout this period: 'A new form for the children receiving parish relief in place of the old cards' (October 1897).

The Poor Law Guardians set a shocking example by sending young children out to work: 'compelling the children whom they relieve as paupers to go to work at Brandon Mill as "Half-Timers". One boy from this school has been forced to go and another child, 8, has been told to go. Both children are fatherless' (April 1872). Later on they took a more enlightened attitude, paying school fees for poor families: 'Annie Rhoads & sisters' school fees are to be paid by the Guardians' (January 1885). However the families of those considered undeserving were penalised through no fault of their own (see box below).

The shadow of the workhouse

'Mrs. M. came crying to-day saying that her husband was in jail & parish relief was stopped. She demanded her children, and said they must go to work' (November 1891). The children, Mary and Eliza, were only ten and six years old; their elder brother Henry (13) was already breaking the law to help make ends meet, being 'employed by one of the Trustees of this school, contrary to the [Education] Act'. To continue the M. family saga, two weeks later the father was: 'out of prison now & out of work, but refuses to go to workhouse'. And who can blame him when a family entering the dreaded workhouse would be split up, fed starvation rations and forced to work for no reward. Over the next few months young Henry continued to truant in order to help support his family, and left to go to work permanently the following year.

An 'Allotment Gardeners' Association' was set up by the local vicar in 1825 on land belonging to the Parish and the Stretton Charities; the rent for a plot was around 7 shillings a year. 'Many children are still absent picking up potatoes for their parents... The mothers get up the potatoes on fine days & of course require their children to pick up. I do not see how this is to be avoided... It is unreasonable to expect the poor to employ labour for which they would have to pay, (even if labourers could be obtained) when they can have the assistance of their own children' (October 1890). Growing corn and vegetables on an allotment helped families to survive irregular employment and low incomes. In 1888 more land was distributed: 'The poor men are to have Mr Quarterman's farm divided among them.'

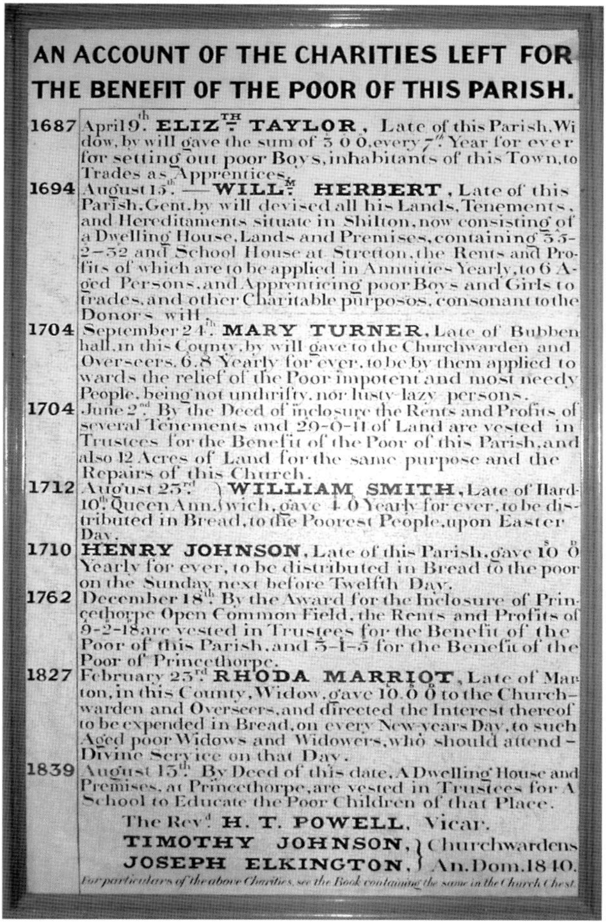

Figure 10

*A board put up in
Stretton Church
in 1840*

> # AN ACCOUNT OF THE CHARITIES LEFT FOR THE BENEFIT OF THE POOR OF THIS PARISH.
>
> **1687** April 19th. **ELIZTH TAYLOR**, Late of this Parish, Widow, by will gave the sum of 5 0 0, every 7th Year for ever for setting out poor Boys, inhabitants of this Town, to Trades as Apprentices.
>
> **1694** August 15th. — **WILLM HERBERT**, Late of this Parish, Gent, by will devised all his Lands, Tenements, and Hereditaments situate in Shilton, now consisting of a Dwelling House, Lands and Premises, containing 3 5-2–32 and School House at Stretton, the Rents and Profits of which are to be applied in Annuities Yearly, to 6 Aged Persons, and Apprenticing poor Boys and Girls to trades, and other Charitable purposes, consonant to the Donors will.
>
> **1704** September 24th. **MARY TURNER**, Late of Bubbenhall, in this County, by will gave to the Churchwarden and Overseers, 6. 8 Yearly for ever, to be by them applied towards the relief of the Poor impotent and most needy People, being not unthrifty, nor lusty lazy persons.
>
> **1704** June 2nd By the Deed of inclosure the Rents and Profits of several Tenements and 29-0-11 of Land are vested in Trustees for the Benefit of the Poor of this Parish, and also 12 Acres of Land for the same purpose and the Repairs of this Church.
>
> **1712** August 25th. } **WILLIAM SMITH**, Late of Hardwich, gave 4 0 Yearly for ever, to be distributed in Bread, to the Poorest People, upon Easter Day.
> **1710** Queen Ann.
>
> **1710** **HENRY JOHNSON**, Late of this Parish, gave 10 0 Yearly for ever, to be distributed in Bread to the poor on the Sunday next before Twelfth Day.
>
> **1762** December 18th By the Award for the Inclosure of Princethorpe Open Common Field, the Rents and Profits of 9-2-18 are vested in Trustees for the Benefit of the Poor of this Parish, and 3–1–5 for the Benefit of the Poor of Princethorpe.
>
> **1827** February 23rd **RHODA MARRIOT**, Late of Marton, in this County, Widow, gave 10. 0 0 to the Churchwarden and Overseers, and directed the Interest thereof to be expended in Bread, on every New years Day, to such Aged poor Widows and Widowers, who should attend – Divine Service on that Day.
>
> **1839** August 15th By Deed of this date, A Dwelling House and Premises, at Princethorpe, are vested in Trustees for A School to Educate the Poor Children of that Place.
>
> The Revd **H. T. POWELL**, Vicar.
> **TIMOTHY JOHNSON,** } Churchwardens
> **JOSEPH ELKINGTON.** } An. Dom. 1840.
>
> *For particulars of the above Charities, see the Book containing the same in the Church Chest.*

Above are listed charitable bequests to support the poor of the parish. In the early nineteenth century they paid for apprentices and aged annuitants, gave soup, bread, furniture, clothes and haircuts to the poor and distributed coal on St John's Day (27th December). In 1859 The Coal Club and The Clothing Club were set up, with rules for eligibility; they offered a savings scheme supplemented by the amalgamated Stretton Charities (the latter still exists). The logbook mentions 'Coal Club week' shortly before Christmas 1895 and 'Mothers to Coventry with Clothing Club Money' (December 1862). The amounts saved could be quite substantial: 'William Clarke whose grandmother is dead & who is going to live with his uncle at Rugby, drew 6/6 out of the Sunday School Clothing Club & 5/- of the Coal Club' (November 1878). A 'Penny Bank' was set up at school in April 1879 to encourage the children to save.

Church and Chapel

The original church became 'ruinous' and was pulled down in the 1830s to be replaced by a new one. The children had a narrow escape on one occasion: 'Yesterday much damage was done to the Parish Church by a violent wind just after dinner time. The greatest amount of debris lay in the two seats where the Sunday School children sat during the Morning Service. Certainly every child would have been killed, had it occurred during the Service' (March 1895). The following year there was a concert in aid of much-needed church repairs.

The Anglican Vicar was a regular visitor to the school, teaching the children scripture, advising the master and certifying the attendance register. The vicars concerned, Henry Wybrow followed by John Richardson, lived in a handsome Georgian vicarage. The vicar's wife and daughters and visiting clergymen would also come to the school on occasions, and sometimes helped out when the teacher was ill. The vicar kept a pig, and when it got out one afternoon six boys were sent off round the village to find it (no doubt glad of the excuse not to study!). In December 1872 the children were taken to church for the 'Day of Intercession for an increase of Missionaries'. From 1862-1870 monthly Missionary meetings were held in the school and the thrifty vicar's wife asked for the candle ends after one such meeting in 1870; five years later oil lamps were first used at the school. We hear of the 'Return of Mr. Wybrow's son from India. Banners, flags &c in honour' (July 1876).

Figure 11   The Anglican Church in Stretton (drawing by Henson Bamford)

All Saints Church, Stretton-on-Dunsmore.

The children were expected to attend Divine Service on Sunday and the master denounced crow-tending (bird-scaring) on the Sabbath (July 1865). They also went with the master to the major church festivals: 'The boys and girls went to church on Ascension day as usual. Many schools have discontinued this practice since the passing of the New [Education] Act' (May 1871). The children also attended marriages of local importance and pupils' funerals: 'Amelia Moss is to be buried this day. School Children took a large wreath of white flowers at 8 o'clock this morning. They made the wreath yesterday under the direction of the Assistant Mistress in the dinner & tea time' (November 1891). The schoolmaster took an interest in the burning religious issues of the day. 'Rev. H. Wybrow called with the petition against the Dis-Establishment of Irish Church' (March 1868). 'Bought a book against Ritualism* at the door' (May 1868).

Figure 12   The Primitive Methodist Chapel in Plott Lane, Stretton (2003)

The early Methodists used a building in the village centre and a tiny Primitive Methodist Chapel was built in 1871, convenient for those living in Poors Plott,* a hamlet on the outskirts of the village. The chapel still survives today, and has recently been converted into a house. 'A Woman was preaching at Stretton yesterday in the open air' (May 1865), presumably a nonconformist, as was the 'Soldier preaching at Faulkner's' in January 1866. The schoolmaster seems to have been tolerant of other denominations: 'Sophia Clarke has returned from the Roman Catholic School at Princethorpe & given up a bead necklace with a pendent cross saying that the "Sisters" told her to burn it if she returned to the Church School. We have not burnt it.'

Crime and Punishment

'George O. murdered his wife at 7 o'clock p.m.' the logbook records with rather hasty judgement on September 22nd 1874. George and Susannah led a quarrelsome life; he arrived back from market and attacked his wife because the kettle was not boiling for his tea. She was heavily pregnant and died in spite of the doctor's efforts to save her. Two of their five children attended school at the time of the tragedy: Sarah (aged three) and Lucy (aged six); two-year old Joseph started a few years later. Lucy had entered school from the workhouse a couple of years previously, so clearly the family was in difficulty at that time. George was found guilty of manslaughter and sentenced to five years penal servitude at Warwick assizes. By 1881 he was out of prison and living with his widowed mother and the three children in the village. Inquests were held in the Dun Cow Inn and the schoolmaster mentions attending one on the body of Mr. H., aged 22. William H. was engaged to a barmaid in Stourbridge whose father wanted half his fortune settled on her; when William declined to do this the engagement was broken off and she refused to see him any more. He took to drink and said he'd never get over it; sadly he shot himself, and was buried on December 4th 1874.

There were cases of child abuse: 'Emma Z., who was lately caught in an indecent position with old Mr. N. & for which he is in prison three months, has returned to school. I fear for the result among my scholars, but trust that God will prevent evil' (June 1879). This reveals a depressingly judgmental attitude towards the victim, though 12-year-old Emma was often in trouble for more childish misdeeds. The logbook also records a wife-beating: 'Mr. C. came to sweep the School this morning instead of Mrs. C. Afterwards heard that he had been ill-using her & she was unable to come out' (October 1876). Men were drunk and disorderly: 'Bob L., a drunken man, chased the school children up to the school, and was nearly causing an accident to the little ones crowding together through the door' (August 1891). The local policeman lived on the London Road.

A reformatory for juvenile delinquents

Warwick County Asylum was an early borstal based at Stretton from 1818 to 1856. Teenage boys at risk of turning to a life of crime were sent by the magistrates to work on the farm for two years and to learn shoemaking or tailoring. They led a Spartan existence, but it was a great deal better than the alternatives (prison, flogging or transportation). The boys used to process in a crocodile over the fields to attend church. The asylum was a considerable success, reforming three-quarters of the inmates, compared with half of an equivalent group sent to prison. Failures included the lad caught by a constable with a dead duck in his possession! Successes included George Wolf, who was transported to Tasmania but made good and had a road named after him.

Transport

Figure 13 The smithy at Eathorpe in the 1900s (photographer H. Elkington)

The main road through the village (now the A45) ran from London to Holyhead via Birmingham and had been made into a turnpike road by Thomas Telford in the eighteenth century. In 1866 the schoolmaster complained about the 11-year-old Haynes boy who was regularly absent minding the tollgate on this road. The 1871 census shows John Haynes, Collector of Tolls, living in Toll Gate House with his wife and grandson, Stephen, the truant concerned. The roads often became impassable in bad weather: the school Inspector was unable to come 'in consequence of the bad state of the roads' in February 1879. Local transport was reliant on horses and there are regular references to waggons, horses and carts: 'Two punished – one for throwing stick at man in coal-cart – the other for shouting at Colonel Powys's pony' (December 1865). The carter, Joseph Falkner, provided a regular service from the village to Coventry on Tuesday and Friday, and to Warwick on Saturday.

Emigration

'George & William Allington withdrawn from school. All the family going to New Zealand' (September 1874). The father, also George, was an agricultural labourer with a wife and five children. This hazardous journey would have taken several months by boat, part of the mass emigration of the working classes that took place between 1871-81, mostly on assisted passages. Not only the working classes went: 'Master went to see his youngest son [22 year-old Ralph Hassall]... set off for the United States of America' (October 1903).

Figure 14 Wolston corn mill in the 1890s; it served Stretton, which had no mill

The railway line from London to Birmingham opened in 1838 and the nearest station to Stretton was at Brandon (2¹/₂ miles away, now closed). Bicycles were invented in 1870 and made locally in Coventry but do not appear in photographs of the village until around 1900.

Communications

The village had a post office throughout the Victorian period. In 1850 White's trade directory reported that: 'Letters arrive by foot-post from Coventry, at half-past 8, a.m. [rather earlier than nowadays!] and are dispatched at 20 minutes after 4, p.m.' Around 1870 the new-fangled electric telegraph was connected to Rugby and Coventry. The master noted: 'I hear that T. Newcombe is implicated in throwing at telegraph wires & breaking the pots belonging thereto' (June 1875); these 'pots' would be the insulators on the poles carrying the wires. The first telephones were not installed in the village until electricity arrived in the 1930s. Systematic mapping of the area was carried out during the nineteenth century and a 1" to the mile map published in 1834. The logbooks report that three children of a soldier employed in the ordnance survey were admitted to Stretton School for a few months in 1884: this must have been the survey that led to the 25" to the mile map (on which Figure 1 is based).

The Weather

The weather had a significant effect on the school; children in the infant school were often kept at home in bad weather: 'Snow coming down fast, very few children at school' (December 1872); 'Very many children came late through sliding on the frozen pond' (December 1879). Some winters were very cold and the ink froze in the pots. In the Great Frost of January 1895 (when Lake Windermere froze over) the master complained of the: 'Glassy state of the roads... The intense cold renders it difficult to keep the fingers sufficiently warm for writing and drawing'. The school was heated by open fires that were clearly inadequate. Wet weather also affected attendance and the master had to dry wet pinafores by the fire on occasions. There was torrential rain in July 1875: 'School doorway flooded, thunderstorms, and lightening prevail. Children's boots soaked by walking through floods on the roads'. The school chimneys were not satisfactory in windy conditions: 'The chimney smoked so badly this morning that the children coughed at their work... we must have a cowl' (October 1873). In the summer it could be very hot: 'Work has been very trying on account of the great heat... 86 degrees in the shade. The children were restless & the atmosphere oppressive' (July 1896 and 1901).

Figure 15 Stretton village green in the snow, 2004
(compare with Figure 2, page 4, taken 100 years earlier)

Conclusion

I hope you have enjoyed this opportunity to eavesdrop on the everyday life of Victorian villagers. We have overheard their gossip, learning about families who prospered and others who were often in trouble. Sometimes the community was shocked by scandal and tragedy when a crime or a death took place. We are indebted to the sharp eyes and ears of the teachers who diligently recorded these events as they happened, over a hundred years ago.

Finding out more
For further reading I recommend Flora Thompson's delightful trilogy *Lark Rise to Candleford* (Penguin, 1973) or some of the material listed opposite. You can visit a Victorian kitchen and schoolroom at St. John's Museum in Warwick. There is also a reconstructed Victorian community at the Black Country Museum in Dudley.

A full transcript of the Stretton School Logbooks (1862-1906), fully indexed by surname, will be available by 2005 in Warwick County Record Office; it will also be for sale on CD for £10 (UK postage included). A transcript of the Stretton School Admissions Register for 1874-92 is available now, price £1.50 (UK postage included); contact details opposite page 1.

Sources and References

This booklet is based chiefly on three Stretton School Logbooks in Warwick County Record Office (reference CR 699/1-3). Other useful sources were:

Brandon Silk Mill: Ghosts of the 11th Green, A. Langley, Stretton Millennium History Group (SMHG) (2001)

Discovering English Customs and Traditions, M. Gascoigne, Shire Publications (2002)

Pleasures and Pastimes in Victorian Britain, P. Horn, Sutton Publishing (1999)

Stretton on Dunsmore: the making of a Warwickshire Village, SMHG (2000)

The Victorian Country Child, P. Horn, Sutton Publishing (1997)

The Victorian Farmer, D. Everleigh, Shire Publications (2002)

The Victorian Schoolroom, T. May, Shire Publications (1999)

Warwickshire Trade Directories, newspapers and censuses of the period.

Acknowledgements

I am very grateful to staff at Warwick County Record Office (WCRO) for valuable help with research and permission to quote extracts from the Logbooks. I would also like to thank the following for permission to publish: SMHG for Figures 1, 4, 6 & 7 (from *Stretton on Dunsmore*) and Roger Clemons who drew Figure 1; Sue Higgins & Dave Bonner for Figure 2; Avril Moore for Figure 11; WCRO, Nuneaton & Rugby Libraries for Figures 3, 5, 13 & 14 from Warwickshire Images (07779, 04009 NL1681, 00913 PH350/2367 & 07848 WWOL725.47) and my mother, Dorothy Wallis, for the cover pictures. Figure 8 is from an old postcard, photographer unknown; I produced Figures 9, 10, 12 & 15. Denise Hume and my husband Peter made helpful comments on this booklet and my daughter Rosemary was a very effective editor.

Glossary

Band of Hope: a temperance movement very active during this period. On joining, young people 'took the pledge' to abstain from alcohol.

Bead-threading: local home-based handwork attaching beads to purses etc. See 'Doing the Beads: By-employment for women and children in rural Warwickshire, 1865-6', M.J. Kingman, *Warwickshire History* Vol X(2) 1996-7.

Gimping: winding silk for trimmings, a local home-working industry.

Godiva: Countess Godgifu's famous nude ride on horseback through Coventry is said to have persuaded her husband, Earl Leofric to waive local taxes; she died in 1067 and Godiva processions were started in the 15th century by Coventry woollen workers.

Guinea: an old unit of currency worth one pound one shilling (£1.05).

Hillies: an area of rough ground opposite the Victorian school including spoil heaps from the gypsum mining that was carried on until the 1900s.

Mop fair: a hiring fair where servants held a symbol of their trade (e.g. a mop).

Oddfellows: a secret benevolent organisation founded in the eighteenth century.

Outdoor relief: money paid to support the poor in their own home.

Penny (d): 1 old penny = $1/12$ shilling = 0.4 new pence.

Penny reading: a public reading from famous authors such as Dickens.

(Poors) Plott: a hamlet built near Stretton for labourers after the Enclosures when labourers lost the right to make use of common land.

Primrose League: an organisation founded in 1883 to support Conservatism.

Ritualism: a high church movement in the Church of England that placed great emphasis on the detail of church rituals.

Shilling (s): a pre-decimal coin worth five new pence (12 old pence).

Statutes: an annual autumn hiring fair and excuse for a celebration.

Tip-cat: a game where a short piece of wood is laid down with one end protruding, tipped in the air and then knocked to a distance with a stick.

Wake: originally a vigil held to commemorate the founding of the local church, but by Victorian times an annual fair; in some districts a factory holiday week.

Wroth Silver: parishes in the Hundred of Knightlow pay their dues to the Lord of the Manor on Martinmas (November 11th) followed by breakfast at a local inn. The ceremony has survived more than 800 years and still attracts a good attendance. See *Wroth Silver Today*, W. Waddilove & D. Eadon (1994).